Selena Perez:
Queen of Tejano Music

Maritza Romero

The Rosen Publishing Group's
PowerKids Press ™
New York

Published in 1997 by The Rosen Publishing Group, Inc.
29 East 21st Street, New York, NY 10010

First Edition

Book Design: Danielle Primiceri

Photo Credits: Cover and p. 8 © Pam Francis/The Gamma Liaison Network; pp. 4, 15 © AP/Wide World Photos; pp. 7, 11 (all photos), 16 © Percy Hawke/Archive Photos; p. 12 © Curt Wilcott/Liaison Network; p. 19 by Seth Dinnerman; p. 20 © Allen/Liaison.

Romero, Maritza.
    Selena Perez : Queen of Tejano music / Maritza Romero.
        p.   cm. — (Great Hispanics of Our Time)
    ISBN 0-8239-5086-7
    1. Selena, 1971–1995—Juvenile literature. 2. Tejano musicians—Biography—Juvenile literature.
I. Title. II. Series.
ML3930.S43R66 1997
782.42164—dc21   97-6730
                                                                 CIP
                                                                 AC

Manufactured in the United States of America

Contents

Los Dinos

Selena Quintanilla was born on April 16, 1971, in Lake Jackson, Texas. She and her family lived in a Mexican American **community** (kuh-MYOON-ih-tee). Music was important to the Quintanilla family, and so was their Mexican **heritage** (HEHR-ih-tej). Selena's father, Abraham, had joined a band when he was in high school. His band was called Los Dinos, or "The Boys." They played a mix of Texan and Mexican music called Tex-Mex. Abraham played with the band until Selena was born. Then he took a job working for a chemical company.

◀ Like her father, Selena loved to make music.

A Young Singer

Although Abraham was no longer in a band, the family played music together. Abraham taught his son, Abraham III, or A. B., to play the **bass guitar** (BAYS gih-TAR). One day when Selena was five years old, she became **jealous** (JEL-us) of the **attention** (uh-TEN-shun) her brother was getting. She picked up a songbook and began to sing. Her voice was strong and she sang beautifully. Her family quickly turned their attention to her.

Selena's family knew there was something special about her singing. ▶

A Cheerful Girl

Selena loved all kinds of music. She began singing country-western songs. Then her father taught her some **traditional** (truh-DISH-un-ul) Mexican songs in Spanish. She learned what the Spanish words sounded like, but she didn't know what they meant. She grew up speaking English. Selena did not learn to speak Spanish until she was an adult. In school, Selena was a good student. She was a cheerful girl. Teachers noticed that she carried happiness and laughter wherever she went.

◄ Selena had a ready smile for her family, friends, and everyone she met.

The Family Band

By the time Selena was nine years old, her father had saved up enough money to open his own business. He quit his job at the chemical company and opened a Mexican restaurant called Papagallo's. The whole family helped out. One of Selena's favorite things to do in the restaurant was to sing. A. B. played bass guitar. Selena's older sister, Suzette, played the drums. And Selena was the lead singer. They played for the customers. Sometimes they played at weddings too.

Selena began singing for small audiences in her father's restaurant. Later she sang for thousands of people at a time. ▶

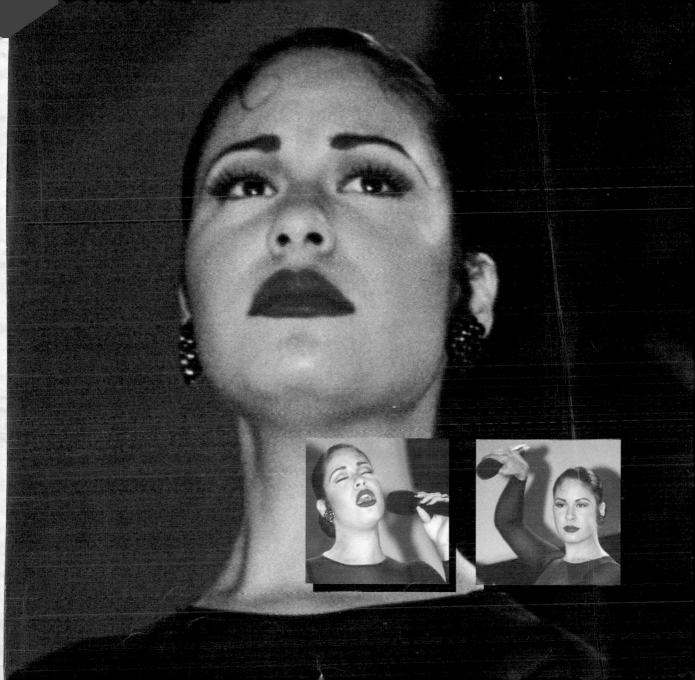

The Quintanillas Move On

Texas is a state where a lot of people have jobs working with oil. Oil is an important **natural resource** (NACH-er-ul REE-sors). In 1981, the price of oil went down, and many of these people lost their jobs. They did not have the money to eat in restaurants anymore. There were not enough customers at Papagallo's. The Quintanilla family lost the money they had spent on the restaurant. They had to close the restaurant and sell their house. The family packed up their things and moved to Corpus Christi, Texas, to look for work.

◄ When the Quintanilla family opened their restaurant, they didn't count on oil workers losing their jobs.

Hard Times

To make money, the family put together a band called Selena y Los Dinos, or "Selena and the Boys." They began traveling around Texas and the Southwest. They played at weddings, in bars, and in clubs. Selena was just ten years old, but she and the band were good. When she was twelve, Selena had to quit school to sing with the band to make money. These were hard times for her family. But the band was so good that in 1983, radio stations began playing their songs. The radio stations liked Selena so much they gave her an award for her singing.

At first, Selena and her family sang to help make money. But Selena kept singing because she loved it. ▶

An Award Winner

Selena and the band played **Tejano** (tay-HA-no) music. Tejano is a mix of Mexican music and **popular** (POP-yoo-ler) music. Many people like to dance to Tejano music. By the time Selena was fifteen, the band was becoming famous. They made several albums in Spanish. In 1986, Selena won the Tejano Music Award for female **vocalist** (VOH-kul-ist) and performer of the year. By 1992, the band had their first hit song, "Buenos Amigos." That same year, Selena married Chris Perez, the band's guitar player.

◀ Selena's music quickly became popular within the Spanish-speaking community.

Selena Becomes a Star

In 1993, the band's record, *Selena Live*, won a Grammy award for best Mexican American Album. Selena had become a star. She loved performing on stage, dancing, and wearing bright costumes. But Selena worked hard off stage too. She visited schools to tell children how important it is to stay in school and to stay away from drugs. She had always dreamed of being a clothing **designer** (dee-ZY-ner). She made that dream come true when she opened two **boutiques** (boo-TEEKS) of her own. She even played a small part in the movie *Don Juan DeMarco*.

Selena gave back to the community that supported her by talking to kids about staying in school and avoiding drugs. ▶

"*Dreaming of You*"

In early 1995, Selena won another Grammy and six Tejano music awards. But tragically, on March 31st, Selena was killed by the manager of her fan club during an argument. She was just about to finish her first album in English, called *Dreaming of You*. Before that, her music had been heard mostly in Hispanic communities. Selena recorded an album in English because she wanted to share her music with everyone. The song "Dreaming of You" was played across the country after Selena's death. That record hit the top of the charts that year.

◄ Selena won several awards, including two Grammy awards, for her music.

A Hero

Selena was a hero to many young Hispanic people. Because she sang in Spanish, she showed her fans that their Hispanic heritage is something to be proud of. As one newspaper reporter wrote, Selena Perez was "a woman of the people." She showed her people, and people everywhere, that it was possible to make their dreams come true, as she had.

Glossary

attention (uh-TEN-shun) Thinking about, looking at, or listening to someone.

bass guitar (BAYS gih-TAR) A guitar that plays the lowest notes.

boutique (boo-TEEK) A small store where fancy clothes are sold.

community (kuh-MYOON-ih-tee) A group of people who live near each other and have something in common.

designer (dee-ZY-ner) A person who plans how something will look.

heritage (HEHR-ih-tej) Cultural traditions that are handed down from parent to child.

jealous (JEL-us) Wanting what someone else has.

natural resource (NACH-er-ul REE-sors) Something that comes from nature that is useful to people.

popular (POP-yoo-ler) Something that is liked by most people.

Tejano (tay-HA-no) The Spanish word for Texan. It is also a kind of music that blends Mexican music with popular music.

traditional (truh-DISH-un-ul) A way of doing something that is passed down from parent to child.

vocalist (VOH-kul-ist) A singer.

Index